AF480561

GET UP, MOMMA

Marqita Brooks

ISBN 979-8-88616-575-3 (paperback)
ISBN 979-8-88616-576-0 (digital)

Copyright © 2022 by Marqita Brooks

All rights reserved. No part of this publication may be reproduced, distributed, or transmitted in any form or by any means, including photocopying, recording, or other electronic or mechanical methods without the prior written permission of the publisher. For permission requests, solicit the publisher via the address below.

Christian Faith Publishing
832 Park Avenue
Meadville, PA 16335
www.christianfaithpublishing.com

Printed in the United States of America

To my lovely daughter Kayla

This story is based on a true story. A year after I gave birth to my daughter, I was diagnosed with type 2 diabetes. I began to have symptoms of fatigue and weight gain caused by depression.

Hi, my name is Kayla, and my momma has type 2 diabetes.

"Momma, can we go to the park?"

"No, baby, Momma is too tired."

"Momma, can we go swimming?"
"No, baby, Momma is too tired."

"Momma, can we go bike riding?"
"No, baby, Momma is too tired."

"Momma, can we go outside and paint?"

"No, baby, Momma is too tired."

I wish my mom didn't have type 2 diabetes so she wouldn't be so tired.

"I wish I wasn't so tired. Maybe I will talk to my doctor."

"Hi, Doctor, I have type two diabetes, and I am always so tired, what can I do?"

"A good diet and exercise could help, and if not, check back with me."

"Okay, Doctor."

5 lb
5 lb
10 lb

"Now that I have been to the doctor, I am not too tired to play at the park, go swimming, go bike riding, and painting outside."

I am so happy my momma is not too tired to play with me.

The End

ABOUT THE AUTHOR

Marqita Brooks is the author responsible for *Get up Momma*. She has a bachelor's degree in applied science. She is a loving mother of one. She has worked with children for over ten years.

To my loving mother, Lorene, and my sweet baby girl Kayla.

www.ingramcontent.com/pod-product-compliance
Lightning Source LLC
Chambersburg PA
CBHW041826110726
48006CB00019B/2530